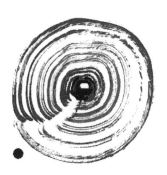

lune 2   LASSAW 1970

THE WIDOW'S
BOOK OF MOONS

a geology of impermanence

Denise Lassaw

Art Work

Drawings by Ibram Lassaw 1913 - 2003: copyright Ibram Lassaw Studio
Untitled pen & ink, 1938, untitled pen & ink 1948,
untitled pen & ink 1966, untitled pen & ink 1967, untitled pen & ink 1970,
Interweave, 1982 pen & ink, untitled pen & link 1984,
untitled pen & ink 1985.
Portrait of Denise, pen, 1962, Sebastian Batanne Matta,1943 - 1976
Protest photo 1990, Linda Smoger, Homer, Alaska
Painted stones, Ernestine Lassaw, 1913 - 2014
Photo's of Alaska and bear - person ink drawing- Denise Lassaw
Cover and book design ~ Denise Lassaw, with the artistry of
InDesign/Photoshop guru, John Lund/Lund Arts, Bellingham,WA

Some of the poems in this book have been published in the following:
What Book!? Buddha Poems From Beat to HipHop, Parallax Press
Whispered Secrets, Sedna Press, Anchorage, Alaska
The Sky's Own Light, poems from Alaska, Minotaur Press
poetryALASKAwomen, Top of the World, Fairbanks, Alaska

copyright: Denise Lassaw 2017

Publisher: Gravity Tension Press
dpaljor@comcast.net

ISBN 978-1542329521

About this book

Long ago in a book of Inuit poems I read, *I am a poor man, I don't know many songs.* Right then I made up my mind to be rich with many songs and stories and I gradually learned to live my life as a good story. This means turning all my experiences into stories as they are happening. I think this ability to step back behind myself as if from a distance, and see things with a mythological or geological eye has saved me when life becomes unbearable. Like everyone else I have had my share of suffering. How are these shares parceled out? I am not claiming to have had either more or less suffering than other people. We each must deal with life as it comes to us or as we create it.

There are a lot of rocks and water in these poems, just as in my life I have lugged rocks from Lake Baikal, Siberia, to Alaska, across Mongolia, from Europe to New York, from Hawaii to Alaska and from New Mexico to New York, and I have abandoned many rocks in all those places because there are only so many rocks one can carry. I love rocks because each rock is a story, like a Rosetta Stone of geologic memory. I love the colors of minerals and the chemistry or alchemy of ceramic glazes and how they change under extreme heat and atmospheres and in relationship to the chemistry of clay bodies. I never actually studied chemistry but I did fire kilns. What I know is mostly from lived experience. Forty-four years in Alaska have given me real experiences with rain, snow, wind, bears, cold, loneliness and great beauty. These poems are also stories. I didn't make them up from nothing. Rocks are created by geologic processes, heat, pressure, water, elements of earth, the same as stars. Our body/minds are made the same way and with the same elements.

Mythology and poetry, shared experiences create an alchemy between people. These poems are an expression of a growing understanding about life. Paljor told me on the first day we met, meditate on impermanence! From a geologic view I understood impermanence but I had yet to really grasp what it had to do with me. Life with Paljor made my synapses light up. I had to adapt to his Tibetan culture and he had to learn to understand America. It was sometimes very difficult for both of us. But where we connected was in poetry and a love of wild nature. Buddhism teaches not only impermanence but interconnectedness and interdependence. You don't need an *ism* to learn this. In the realms of highest physics and biology scientists have come a long way towards poetry, each expressing reality in their own language. When I read books on systems theory and how all living and non-living things are interdependent I feel solidly connected. Feeling connected in a really large way propels me beyond the impermanence that is myself, but also brings me back to all the ways that human life is a poem. A drop of water can awaken a seed and a flower can call a butterfly, one story generates another, and with a little grace, beauty is born.

These poems were written after Paljor's sudden death on October 25th, 1988. They explore the process of my grief, understanding of impermanence, and a curiosity about the whole journey. I hope the reader will see that these elements dance together with a smile.

Denise Lassaw 2016

Contents

THE WIDOW'S BOOK
OF MOONS

a geology of impermanence

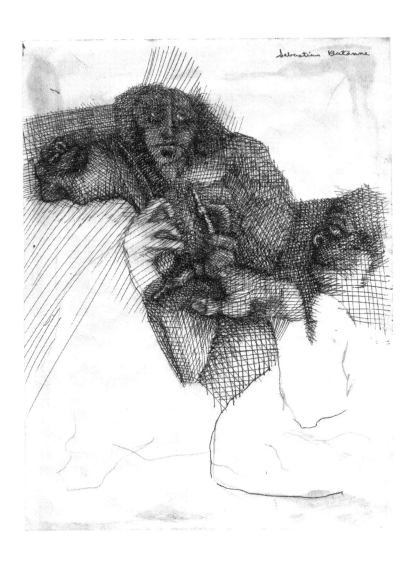

Rolling Down in Berries

Berries
      I love you
              berries
rolling down
         rolling in berries
Laughing
blueberries cranberries
gray mist on black rock cirque
cranberries are tart before deep frost
I touch you gently sweet blueberry
carefully pluck you from your nest of ruddy leaves
my berries

The wet chilly wind
fireweed gone red leaved   alder all yellow
deep green sponge of black crowberries
I kiss you
roll in your springy bed
Hudson Bay tea smells spicy in damp moss
My face buried in your hair

Alpine berry reds and rubies where the granite bones protrude
mica shimmering rivulets flowing   plat plat plat
nosily carving the bank of moose-berries sweet decay

Blue spaces in purple clouds
black-haired berry eater   blueberry mouth
you press me warmly   deep in berry carpet
eagle plays the high currents of air
berry kisses raindrops caught in cloud berries cupped leaves

we roll down
        down
           roll down
                laughing

    be-berried

Chugach Mountains, September 1988

Ngondro Practice

One hundred thousand flower petals
One hundred thousand stars
One hundred thousand snow flakes
One hundred thousand tears

your photograph amid the candles
a finger raised *in delight*
        that naughty smile

O! so *this*   is impermanence

within an altar of flowers
your brightness lies perfumed in light
flowers glow like stars   each one
a jewel-like passage to Buddha-fields
        uncountable

tears like stars falling   each tear
a poem
        shining alone in blue night
the delicate flowers of your friends love
are all   are all
        that hold you here

if my tears became stars
the night would blaze
        with a hundred thousand colors
O my beloved
        I offer you that night

1st Moon Anchorage

Icebound Whales
at Point Barrow Escape

*Day after day you followed their story in the Daily News. Your heart
swelled with compassion for the icebound whales.*

Great grief came over me
today you freed the whales

Locked in narrow channels
you were locked in this body

Great grief came over me
my beloved has freed the whales

They swim in open waters
you swim in a sea of shooting stars

Great grief came over me
I was not set free

1st moon Anchorage

Second Night

The fabric of the universe has ripped
nothing holds its place
tears   stars   snowflakes
have lost their names and fall
fall effortlessly as living jewels
in this blackest night beyond time

O living beings
let me carry your grief and pain
my heart has expanded beyond breath
my load is already the weight of the galaxy
nothing can crush me more

I have entered the center of all pain

O great buddhas and bodhisattvas
I offer to you the energy
of this suffering
may it be transformed
into Dewachen and bless Paljor

1st Moon Anchorage

Blue Dawn 4 November

At the door of the infinite   I looked back
only one step away from Beauty
my mind hesitated
                I lost you forever !

Your true face of compassion invited me   a presence of love
among the pink clouds of the Horse-Head nebula
blue and white stars pulsed brilliantly within your translucent mouth
your eyes   deep as black holes
absorbing all   colors of light   penetrated me with rosy love

Drawn into space   my open heart a magnet   attracted by pink light
lifted   like a feather from my warm bed   I flew towards you
pulled outwards among the stars by the thread of my heart
reaching out to join you in a garden   trees and
flowers   glowing in colors unknown to me
delicate plants of pure light

Your misty face dissolved into the nebula
I was standing alone in a narrow door frame
hanging in space   no walls no floor only space
only the universe wholly present spinning   across time
and I   tethered like a kite in a sky without wind
held by a thin line
I had reached the door of decision   and
could go no further as a drifter

I looked out

In 10 directions space stretched endlessly
watching my own spiral galaxy
like a spider's web rippling in a great slow dance
I saw the width of the cosmos as closely as the furrows of my hand
the dimensions of this living being   a myriad of solar systems
garden planets   spread before me

I felt it   this living force so huge   so huge
I trembled in awe   my mind
could not contain it

Everywhere at limitless distances galaxies pulsed and flickered
in diamond sharp colors
I saw all of time across space   the immensity of it
I staggered dizzily from a reality that was too great for me

Knowing then that all journeys are made alone
no promises can be kept   no one path
I understood that to step out here
would be to sever my human life
I   would not return
an image came to me beyond words   a responsibility
came to me and its voice was clear
my own mind whispered   *Who will do this work*
Who   will do this work?
                          meaning everything
my life

There was no moment of stillness
no time   no time
I fell backwards with great force
pulled as if my elastic cord had passed
its limit and reeled me in violently
I awoke   hair standing on end
awoke
tears streaming from my human eyes

At the door of the infinite   I looked back
only one step away from Beauty
my mind hesitated
          I lost you forever!

1 moon Anchorage

Jigme's Grief 11.4.88

Feeling your absence Jigme wanders
from room to room
when I awake at night he is there
watching
he cries in the day
waiting at your closed door
he cries
I open the door to the shrine
still crying
he circles round your pillow
and drapes his orange body
in the place you kept warm

1 Moon

Tiny Sweets

I nibble on your little bones
beloved   my dearest
like tiny sweets
          in a bowl
absently   I eat your bones
          and stare
across the table
          a strange land
s u s p e n d e d
          in
              time

You

You are
The eye that knows itself
Kinetic layers of the earth
Blue sky, white clouds
Blazing stars
Apart from no-thing
Magnetic force
Uncurling leaves
The sound of glaciers
Calving into the sea
Your form
Returned to all forms
Never was
Never was

Never was lost

Swoyambhu

In bright moonlight

we slide   down Swoyambhu mountain

down the metal banister

in white moonlight

air   thick

alive   between us   never touching

but joined by the night

you a monk   robes flowing   laughing

myself a woman   touched

by the shape of space   and joy

gliding down the long stairway

we pass 2000 year-old stone goddesses

wrapped in the strong roots of trees

I too am wrapped

in the sweet milk of the moon

which is love

without holding on

to anything

Swoyambhu moon

Swoyambhu moon

the monkeys sing in their dreams

   slide on

          slide on

              slide on

7 Moons, Kathmandu, Nepal

Prisoner

In the depth of the beveled mirror
your image
      from the corner
           of my eye
always
    just slipping
        away

so many years
    your reflection next to mine
It must be the mirror's habit
to reflect you

should I break the glass
    because it makes me cry ?

10 Moons Anchorage

His Flute

On the mountain
where your breath once gave
this bamboo flute sweet sound
I build a stone house
              for your bones
Trying   trying
         to make a sound
 Hair pulled
              straight out in the wind
Tears
        blown away to sea
I think to smash this stubborn flute
         and raising it over the stones
Like a sacrifice
              SUDDENLY
It shrieks and wails
         O my beloved
              How can I kill this flute
That is so faithful
         To you

Last Home Coming

The geese you loved
Are wandering
Amid wind-torn clouds
     Beloved
Like them I journey
     with intent
Strangers will bear you
Home
       to Chomalungma

And offer these
Dry ashes
     that often dreamed
The flight of geese
To the highest snows
And the blues
Of vast
      wind-polished space

12 moons

So Much

I don't wait for the moon
but in deepest night
the Moon
            waits for me

glaring into dreams
illuminating mountain ranges
each fold   and shadow

until I feel ashamed
to sleep
            with so much
                        beauty shining

One Year

I dream of going to meet you
So happy   so happy
Which of us has been away ?
Gray snow was falling that day
I've missed you
            I want to tell you   everything

Your name in crushed snow

One year
I tear the red petals out   they f a l l
Drops of bright blood
            In white snow

You're here ! Where are you?

One year
The driver didn't see
Two flowers standing alone
Sky clear   sea silken with cold

O n e   year
A barrier is between us !
I can't find you
Now there is silence   no sirens   no ships
No workers   only two red flowers
And drops of blood   my tears
I awake and remember
You are dead
One year

13 Moons

This Little Bone Visits the Night

This little bone asked to visit the night
The moon being almost full and
Temperature about zero
This little bone wanted
To know the night   the wind
The silver light of the night
This tiny bone cried out

Carry me in the night !

The snow crunching deep   like
A field of stars enfolding us

Ah   said the little bone
I remember the night

Shall I take you out of your box?
I asked the little bone

Ah   let the wind blow through
My hollow place   how cold
How vast   the space of night
When you're a bone   even a tiny one
You really feel things   closely

Yes I said I feel the cold very closely

That's not how I mean said the little bone
You feel cold outside you feel the depth
Of space   apart   But I am truly hollow
The night passes within me   on both sides

I'm getting frostbit I said
We have to go home

Too bad   said the little bone
I wouldn't mind

being left out here . . .

But I would miss you too much   I told him
And besides It amuses me to think
You   a tiny bone
Were once my husband

15 Moons Knob Hill

When You Died

There was no earth to stand on
No movement
No death
No hunger
No need of dreams
No breath
No sound
When you died
There was no pain
No tears
No realization of anything
No time
No mind
There was only heat   intense heat
Wave after wave   crashing
        wave after wave
All consuming
W h i t e   h e a t

Then
When I opened the furnace door
And stepped out
The fabric of the universe
Hung in tatters
And the cats were hungry

16 Moons Knob Hill

Geranium

I am a universe

e x p l o d i n g

      with pain

and yet

      I grow flowers

HA !

      if you only KNEW

the FEROCIOUS power

      hidden

          and bridled here !

this soft

coral-petaled geranium

would

      TERRIFY you !

Stamp My Foot

I am the universe
Being cut
With a Diamond Sword
The pain of this wound
Sears my flesh
But I can not die
Nor refuse
      To s u f f e r
I   who   CELEBRATED
Every color and form
Who welcomed EVERYTHING

Like a galaxy e x p a n d i n g

In delight

I STAMP MY FOOT

I STAMP MY FOOT

and HOWL

17 Moons Knob Hill

Dead Flowers

Why do I pull dead flowers

Off the vine ?

Their bodies like the wings of moths

Have no bones no blood

Dried flowers   hanging

by a withered stem

Pale brown and delicate

They remind me of impermanence

I also shall crumble

Into dust

That is certain

But

    Will I flower ?

Poet's House

In the house of the cranes

In this land of loons

I wait for you

In the place where the bear's

Footprint sucks down the mud

Still swirling

This wide sky   Beloved

I offer to you

20 Moons Knob Hill

7.5.90 Dream:
Paljor asks me for his book of poems

I was climbing a tall wild mountain. Its peaks were sharp, glaciers of blue light vanished into the sky. It was *very* high. I followed the earthy-rocky trail and then ladders that passed up through tunnels. or brightly colored metal tubes about six feet in diameter, filled with light. One of the tubes was painted Chinese yellow, as if it were part of a children's playground. Each place the ladder ended there were small log cabins. I reached a place where the air was thin and cold. I wasn't dressed for climbing a real mountain. I had only jeans and light a sweater. No boots. But I wasn't worried. Going up was easy, and I climbed confident that I would reach the top of this dangerous mountain. As I came up to a new level I found Paljor and Lydia and some other friends. They were concerned about me, climbing so unprepared. They each gave me socks, mittens, hats etc. Some were very colorful ones that I had knit myself. I chose those and a Tibetan hat with fur and beautiful rainbow colored wool. Paljor gave me a book about a *paper-book-plant*, like a Field Guide, so I would recognize the plant and collect it on the top of the mountain. He asked me to bring him *his share* of the paper plant. I felt a deep concern and intense-physical presence of love from him. Then I woke up. Now I understand that he wants me to publish his book of poems as we had planned in 1987. But it is only after I have made this dangerous journey. His *share* is what tells me that I am also collecting paper for myself. Does the special paper come from Tibet or is the completion of the journey what transforms ordinary paper into the mountain paper? There are no plants growing on the top of sky-piercing mountains, but I have to go to the top to get the paper. So this makes a difficulty. Will I know when the time in right?

22 Moons Knob Hill

Note: The next year when I was in New York I visited some Tibetan friends who had a shop on Thompson Street. As a present they asked me to choose a hat. There was the hat of my dream: hand woven rainbow colored wool with thick black fox fur. A few years later in Nepal I discovered that there is a plant that grows in the mountains called the paper-book plant. Twenty eight years later I have just published Paljor's *Songs of a Wild Yak*, alas on ordinary paper.

Twenty-two Moons

This sad music
        this constant soft rain
my dying cat
only remind me you are gone
my women's body aches
        for your love

22 moons since you died
I let a stranger take me
        I was laughing
crying
washing this body in midnight
        pacific ocean
unfaithful to you this once

cloud covered in tall grass
in a house
of sad music and blue windows
I wait
        for a cat to die
        for love to part the grass
can you forgive me
        these unfaithful thoughts?
my dear dead one

For Nyima the cat
22 Moons Knob Hill

25

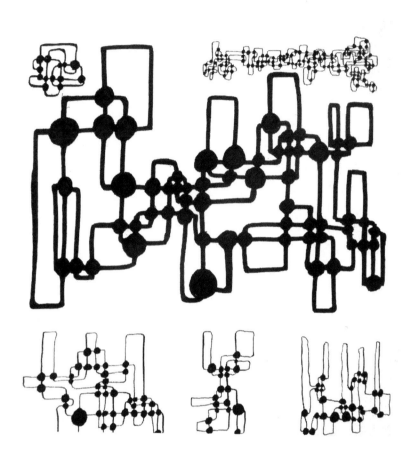

Hunter

Dream is my hunting ground
Incubated under sedimentary layers
Of memories and quilts
I follow faint scents
Through high hills
Ocean currents and
The vast spaces between stars
Hunting   hunting   for you
If I've found your footprint
In mud or cloud
I feel closer than ever
But most often
I return
Reluctantly
Empty handed   and hungry

22 Moons Knob Hill

27

You Have Nothing to Fear

My arms are powerful
Like Hanuman the Monkey King!
I open my chest
And show my faithful heart
To the rising moon.

Shoreline

The sky opens

River of clarity

Between purple banks

Without fish or rocks   sand or mud

This river has no waves

Only an abyss of blue light

Now filling with stars

24 Moons Knob Hill

A Gift

You are the edge of space
the cutting blade of suns
the radiant burn   the deepest black
of black holes
a gift to me your death
kicked me out
into great intensity
the compassion of pain
is bliss

I have everything !
wind   ice   shining stars
a long empty road
breath   song
tears enough for glacial snow

MIND
holding everything
within love's circle
all pervasive
the deep booming beat
of my hero's heart
you
are the edge of space

Orpheus Regrets

On the edge of the galaxy
I turned
And looked back
Now tears flow
And flow
I should have gone
With you

Your true face
A shimmering mist
Suns pulsing pink and blue
Below my feet
       light-years
Vast spiral galaxies awe-some play
Behind me
The door to human dimensions

On the edge of the galaxy
I turned   I turned
On the edge of the galaxy
I fell back

25 Moons Knob Hill

Torma Offering

O let me dance
        on the crystal blades of stars
penetrated with passion by wisdom's sword
mind cut in light
body an offering to the hunger
never filled
I would dance to the end
      of every passion
      creation   endless bliss
destroyed
      dissolved

25 Moons Knob Hill

Organization

Make a list
Of what you should do
Of things to be avoided
Of attitudes to transform
Make a list
Of what needs moving
Of love that needs making
Make a list
Put numbers on tears
On stars
On flowers
List the sorrows of the world
Your own sorrows   then
Throw away all the lists
Experience JOY

27 Moons Knob Hill

34

First Days

I thought I could remain

In bliss

On the razor's edge of grief

But without food   without sleep

I felt   n o t h i n g

To feed grief's alchemical fire

I ate and slept

And so

I have not been

Entirely consumed

Regretfully

I will live

I will

live

27 Moons Knob Hill

Where Do Things Go
When They Are Lost?

All atoms now existing
have existed since mind
moved or
              before
circulating forms
              in the non-dual universe
metamorphic sedimentary DNA
slipping past us   us slipping   past us

the flowers honey-bee-bird-cat
cloud-seed-leaf-rabbit-fox-rock   a cool wind holds
the smell of the sea

Don't worry so much !
         Can anything really be lost
                  except car keys and socks?

Look how beautiful things are !
Who were they yesterday ?
These clouds
         these bones   these lost dreams and poems
they are here   transformed

The moon is laughing at your silver mirror
but   please
watch carefully for the absence of light
in my   reflection

Odysseus's Advice

Sometimes a path opens before you

where there is no ground to walk on

in a strange direction

a path of brilliant beauty opens

suddenly at your feet

and there's no time to consider

or to consult anyone   or say goodbye

and you are naked

if this should ever happen

as you are sitting still

or walking out the door

or in a dream

then focus your heart-mind fully

on the sweet clarity that invites

don't look back

just go   just go on

trust in beauty

step out !

Silence

the moon slips

like a rosy tear

sinking down

cloud hidden volcano's sides

utter stillness

gray blue sky-land

not even

the faint print of bird claws

break deep snow

29 Moons Knob Hill

Holding You Again

My sweet, my beloved now four years gone
when will you stop defining my life?
I am burning with a passion
for the blade of Manjurshi's sword
just cut me up in little pieces
and feed me to the birds
you've taken rebirth   that's fine for you!
What about my life?
I'm still missing the you who was
and now I can change your diapers
how do you think I feel?
you look at me   big eyes   saucy wise smile
holding you to the mirror
you look at me   not yourself
and   I can't look at all
my white hair showing

42 moons Dharamsala, India

Uaarrghh

Uaarrghh! Uaarrghh!

     Whose breath going out ?

My hair rises   I suck in air

     Uaarrghh!

        sounding from deep

within the alder thickets dim green light

     twisted branches

My heart beats faster

     I grab my axe

and quickly ducking low

     scramble away

Uaarrghh! Uaarrghh!

Bear breathes out

  I breathe in

     g r a t e f u l l y

sharing the air

45 Moons Knob Hill

Slip Between the Folds

The sandhill cranes vanish

into the folds

of the rolling land of clouds

their voices follow them

at a distance

cold wind

       bright sky

I too might slip away

just slip away

very slowly

deep in the roots of the tall hollow grass

warm in the tangle of old roots

laying so still

grass and wind would weave my form

and I would slip away

       and leave only

             an empty shell

                 of matted yellow grass

Your Image

That

m o r n i n g

I filled my eyes

with   you

n o w

almost four years

to the moon

your   image

burns   in

my mind

What Remains?

You died. What remains?
I gave it all away
    clothes to the homeless
          glasses to monks
                    money to your family
poems to the world
your father's silver tea bowl
  I gave
          to a living Buddha
your ashes and bones spread
          on mountains and deserts
hidden in holy places
  offered to glaciers
          cast into streams
                    lakes and oceans
you died
what remains?
now multi-formed
          there is more of you
everywhere
your teachings fill my bones

from this beating heart
          I thank you
for your great love
          I thank you
in death you taught me
how suffering
          is transformed to bliss
nothing is left
but
          Thank You

I am Flying

1
The sea is glass   I am flying
translucent blues a fabric
of glass threads undulating with breath
alive over earth's fault lines
flying I see it all   mountains   curved valleys
glacial grooves cloud cities
the roll of hills all bound tight
transparent warp weft time I
am flying   and the sea is silk and glass
2
Sea weaver
blue gray white   silver-green
winter sea seduces
white red brown black coal seams on cliffs
fabric of snow spruce patterns
on jumbled hills
from my flying eyes
transparent layers are understood
wind's hands smooth the bay
calm
beneath   a hidden passion

3
silver gray green clear
waves combing threads of jeweled light
rough silk icy sea caresses
black coal sand snow creek mouths know
the icy roll of pebbles
spruce-black patterns quilt the hills
the blue eye of sky space
fault lines veins of volcanic fingers
a million years opens like a flower
eye-flying-mind-body
threaded across the wind's warp

descends and stops
unbuckle seat belt
walk
but the taste
of light remains

Your Weight

When flesh has been stripped
off the bones of the cloud
and the tree's sap all sucked dry
When all the camouflage confetti
has been shaken in agony from my mind
and at 3 A.M. SUDDENLY
your picture falls off the wall
I can tell you plainly beloved
you are five years dead
Won't you admit it?

When will the cataclysm of your death
become as insubstantial as the fragrance of your socks?
All the mystical jewels of your life have become
too heavy for me
I have to choose to carry me or carry you
We must decide   beloved   Who died in 1988?
Are you sure it was me?

Sometimes it seems I have lived your death
better than I have lived my life
could anyone ask for a more faithful wife?
So when can I stop keeping lists
of things to tell you?

How can you be in two places at once ?
If you are reborn in Dharamsala
why are you still in me?

60 Moons Knob Hill

For a Moose on Paljor's Death Day
10.25.93

Snow twirling night road
within a breath's space
one life   one life gone
covered with moose hair   glass and blood
a moment flashed in darkness   returned to light
impermanence sharper than the blade of seconds
cut between us
would I have known   if   light
            had not returned?
Did you?

Now I understand
in that time
      there is no fear
            no indrawn breath
only clarity
and the result of actions

mind is without borders
skin is no defense against steel
this was the death of flesh
now becoming food
do Moose minds return to willows?

O great Bodhisattva moose
all sentient beings
thank you
for life

61 Moons Knob Hill

Reality One O One

The moon has no light of its own!
Sat Chit Ananda!
red sun - red moon
rolling on gravity's radius
red sun sets - red moon rises
they are flawless

Ankle deep in new snow
I empty the compost bucket
onion skins   old rice   carrot tops
who will eat them
by the moon's borrowed light ?

The sky field is luminous blue
I make gasho
to everything

61 Moons

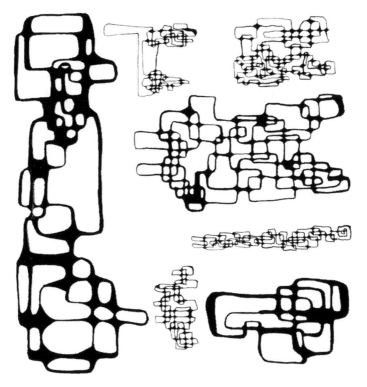

Arakelian 1967

Snow

snow knows the shapes things dream of themselves
morphic resonance intuited in water crystal
thickening branches graying
the green-blackness of spruce trees
snow falling snow falling   breathless
four days I watched
rocks and bushes grew rounded   huge
blending their shapes in whiteness
a unity of atomic truth
dead flowers under snow's tender weight
        like sleep filling the spaces between rose thorns
            binding spruce arms to the earth
                bowing the alder's resilient branch
four days I watched snow fall
and then
I sweated a path through deep powder
uncovering my existence
        with a red shovel
            so
yesterday the truck stood on four black tires
yesterday there was a road for journeys
yesterday the world demanded my attention

but

            all night

trees moaned their longing to fly

my log house shook

while drifting snow filled in

        the trails and traces of my work

           all sign of my life vanished

as morning opens in wild brilliance

I am pulled   as if by magnets

into the whirlwind of crystals

        putting on my skin of padded feathers

          I go out

in the middle of the snow garden

joining all else

      I sink   submissively

        into the heart of the storm

laying motionless

      on this wind-become-earth

         the snow

            will shape me into dreams

Kerulin

Hot marmot grease runs down my chin
Kerulin river smooth flowing   clear
with grandchildren of Genghis Khan
I sit in grass whose roots fed his horses
700 years among flowers   the marmot ate
today I wash down this wild flower meat with
kumis   milk of fat mares grazing among us
the damp earth smell of high country
chilly evening August stars unchanged
since Genghis camped here as a boy
this is how it feels to be human

Kerulin River, Hentii Mountains, NE Mongolia 1994

The Way Snow Falls in Homer

The snow is falling endlessly drifting and blowing   gently hovering
descending slowly to gather in huge round lumps enlarging branches
graying the blackness of spruce trees   filling the spaces under the
trees   catching the lowest branches every day snow snow falling
without stopping   without breathing   truck disappears   shovel
vanished under snow   cat pees on the bathroom floor says snow
too deep for me   goes back to sleep then we fight over chairs
my favorite is his also   lamp over computer table is his sun
mouse pad his bed   office chair his watch tower but I spin
him around   he retires to basket chair- for now, a truce.
Radio says snow for tomorrow   14 foot waves on the sea
gale warning Gore Point to Kamishak Bay
8 point earthquake near the Aleutians, small earthquake
early this morning rocked my bed   snow is still falling
some ships on the sea went down everybody saved oil spill
on pipeline bigger than reported   the wind was blowing
so hard they couldn't see how much oil spilled small
malfunction of small electronic something
Snow hangs like a veil dimly covering my eyes covering sky
mountains lower forest sounds and stars   world politics
Tibet handsome Amdowa's sorrows changing edges to
roundness I feel sleepy and would drift under the whiteness
and impermanence of snow mindless and warm under the
soft soft white beautiful sweet snow

The harbor master says people please check your boats
some are sinking due to the weight of the snow some cats are
lost others have been found a dog on East End road is vicious
will the owner come get it a horse is loose drivers on Diamond
Ridge beware to Mountain Mama visitors arriving tomorrow
weather permitting waves too big today got the engine parts
to Clem at Halibut Cove baby girl arrived last night 7 pounds
5 ounces all doing well save some dandelion wine for us!
Radio keeps us above the snow connected to the unseen
others who are buried in the distance like bright moons
invisible beating hearts   hidden under the whiteness
Snow blowing drifting in wide curves
the blue shadows of the cut edge Snow.

75 Moons Knob Hill

What I Really Want to Say at the Minerals Management Meeting Tonight

This salmon body halibut soul seal home wears no man's name
These living waters fed by volcanic snows and ash spruce alder
willow grass lands
muddy runoff blueberry bog eagle's nest and moose home
existed before COOK INLET
Named for one tired human being who wandered in deep waters
With brass looking glass and pen
This watershed bio-region-great-life-force is not a resource bank for your money,
or a National anything
What nation dares place small name and numbers on a dance
of interconnectedness so vast it is beyond anyone's comprehension!

Hey listen you crazy greed-oriented lost bodhisattva of industrial mind
Just STOP Everything Now   Stop! Stop! Stop!
Stop all this waste and polluting destructive activities
Get-a-hold-of-yourselves   and listen   Slow down clowns
These volcanoes are pulsing pure love in the grinding of continental plates
Let that oil lie greasing the wheels of the planet
Sit still and listen to the salmon sing, the wind blow the cottonwood
sweet spring rotten alder melting sun warmed amid dead leaves

Your greed is killing the web... But honey-child YOU are not the spider
I just want to tell you... You are only a dew drop on the web of life...
I say stop! Stop your madness, WAKE Up to the flight of Stellar's jays'
blue flash and laughter   You can't replace the morning poems of ravens
with money
Money doesn't exist   it is only a game
and I say you also are non-existent   Not Independently existing to eat
the whole planet for some abstract something called money

Money is not worth the death of delicate and invisible plankton
I am talking about something that is curved and slippery
and multi-dimensional, and doesn't fit on Cost-benefit analysis spread sheets
LIFE itself- raw and bigger than your greed covered numbers

STOP EVERYTHING! SHUT UP! SIT DOWN!
BREATHE and
WAKE UP! WAKE UP!
WAKE UP!

78 Moons1995

Read at a Minerals Management Meeting in Homer, Alaska

Kachemak Bay Dzogchen

All sentient beings are my mothers. Tides go out, go out. They rise. Moon rises.
All sentient beings have been my mothers, my relatives. One ocean is going in,
out, moving by the moon, but all sentient beings continually are my mother.
Sentient beings change but Mother does not change. The Moon and I dance
with all beings, one ocean licking the shore. O Mother!
Ravens, Stellar's jays, spruce trees, sea cucumbers.
The moon knows this and the ocean comes in, comes in.
Otters. Whales. Moose. Coyote. Mountain Ash.
The ocean goes out out out but the moon is in all of us.
We are family. Air. Water. Wind. Sun. Fire. Ice. Grass.
The grass waves in the wind while blue tides walk the land like salmon.
Children play in the shallow water. Stones roll under the waves when the tides
come in. Whales sing in the ocean, in the blue bay. Fireweed feathers. The silver
tide goes out, goes in. All sentient beings. I am my mother. Bears eat salmon.
Sun eats the moon. Moon tides run out out out. Sun rises. It is always day
always just before pink dawn.

We are our mothers. Salmon gives birth to bear. Willow births moose. I am bear
mother opening my legs to the tides. They go out, go in. I give seed to berries.
Bear cubs play in the shallow water. Salmon swim into willow roots. Sandhill
cranes smell the moon and dance. Geese eat grass. All sentient beings Are. All
sentient beings- those with mind, those with breath, those whose eyes reflect
the star tides. Our mother moon tastes the tides with tongues of light. Clear
blue, bright green, the color of leaves and tears. Rocks roll roll in her body,
she tastes their sentience. She is our mother, you are mine, and I give birth to
ravens song. Mountains are great mothers to us. Mountains call snow. Salmon
know the taste of waters. They smell their mother's body rolling in the tides.
Our selves, our mothers, all sentient clouds flying in waves. Clear water rises
from the sea to rain the mountains green.
Wild roses. Wolves. Rabbits. Dandelions. Mice.
Porcupines, our prickly mothers.
The clouds bring the sea to them. Salmon swim to them through the sky.
Mountains call them, our mothers all.

Soundings

The clear salty water at the sound of a bell
comes gently without hesitation against the rocks
a slowness that can penetrate rocks, atom to atom
moss grows at the meeting place
this vibration   this breath of water   air
birds chirp   the pulsing of a moth
passes faintly   leaves ripples fanning out
to fade in the water like mirrored light
like a last breath let go
there is no resistance   everything moves naturally
inward and outward
among the many layers of possible minds

BONG! ok.

79 Moons   China Poot Ba

Secret Language

The lost   ummm   sound
the lost ah and ooh
the lost Sanskrit root at 2 A.M.
the lost growl
          a lost brown hand
                    a sneeze
deep chanting   a lost laugh
lost the pronunciation of Sphinx repeated
repeated until
          enlightened giggles consumed us both
lost   black hair as thick as a horse's mane
          the texture of it against my breast
lost   the seed for children
lost a certain   uncertain future
connections   forms of script   an angry word
lost   an entire universe of one mind
lost memories that   were never mine
lost alphabets   lost black eyes
lost by *ACCIDENT*
          lost by karma

Forced to the Edge

I'm not fool enough to yell
HOW DARE YOU ! at the universe
Why waste my breath while stars are forming
These ashes and bone dust
whose are they anyway
            yours or mine?

My voice has been clipped like bird's wings
            and my eyes are full of bay water
Don't ask me to sing you a sad song
            when the roots of language are rotting into mulch
I would become seaweed or dry grass in fall
let the wind be my voice
            and bury these amber tears like treasure books
where only the fish can read them

Some other universe, some other planet

you can cheat on me and I'll overlook it

but don't expect this bodhisattva to forgive blueberries

for dreaming of bears' tongues

I can't dance in an incoming tide

let me sit on a high rock

and just follow the grain..

it's an old pattern handed down since Eve

planted her own garden

if there's a path around here somewhere

I'll find it!

Morning weight - Jigme

Blue dawn deep sleep
I feel the weight of you across my back

I do not feel rain soaked fur
I know nothing of dead mice in my slipper

Pink dawn
My neck is pressed into the pillow
Soothed by a vibrant warmth

Yellow dawn
I dream my head is on fire
I am caught   pinned smothered

White day
Perfume of wet cat envelopes me
All my dreams are true
I struggle to shake free

And then I hear
Feed me meow meNOW

82 moons Knob HIll

65

Process

The sun slips backwards across our mountain horizon
points jagged in dark silhouette sky golden and gray
so summer slips past us
                    leaves turn yellow
and I enter my 50th year going forward forward
without you my beloved
O I have turned an angry eye away from your picture
you unfaithful one gone beyond
gone beyond
seven years I have kept your memory bright
carried this flame against the wind
now alone beyond loneliness, beyond anger
watching the crumbling of things sweeping the dust
not even the vast sky can save me
and the wind blows ceaselessly. . .
who will carry my light into the wind?

84 Moons Knob Hill

Sun and Moon Embrace

Willow stems are reddening
along the river bank
overflow ice shattered
brown water brown earth
red buds of alder
something irrepressible takes hold
I feel our yearnings
this deep blush of desire
my body's aching
in fattened stem and bud
rosy-willow-penises swollen
with lust for spring

Where does it come from
this great longing to burst
open into leaf or song ?

Desiring to press firmly
my fingers like thin roots
seeking fertile darkness
in warming earth

Even rocks are not unmoved
and this all encompassing
liberation of sensuousness
greening and liquid
extends beyond horizons
stars brighten
as if filled
with pungent spruce resin
We have been caught singing
at the instant of dawn
in a radiant joy fusing
silver sun and full golden moon

90 moons Knob Hill

Appearances

Don't let the cool sky of evening
fool you
the land is burning
with a passion for fire

I talk well, telling
pleasing stories
but on the other side of mind
there is a rasping desire
a loneliness
not filled by earth or sky

93 Moons Knob Hill

I See You

I see you
        Bouncing up mountains laughing

I see you
        Playing a bamboo flute in the rain near blue glaciers

I see you
        Holding a large spoon like a magic wand while the soup is boiling

I see you
        Wondering why the car won't start why people like you why
        freedom
        is not easy

I see you
        Meditating in dim light cedar smoke fills the air

I see you
        On your beloved red mountain bike

I see you
        Burning the name of your eldest sister not the first death

I see you
        With your dictionaries on a long wooden table Sanskrit Pali
        Tibetan
        Korean Thai English two celadon cups and a steaming pot of tea

I see you
        Black hair tickling me as we roll in flowers unseen

I see you
        That last morning eating oatmeal

I see you
        Looking seriously far away as you walk out the door

I see you
        Wrapped in plastic and white sheets
                I cannot unwrap you they say

I see your hands
            In a photograph   I miss them
I see your mouth moving in my dreams
            but I can't hear the words
I see your crushed body
            While I explain to your old mother why I have traveled
            5 thousand miles alone
I see you
            In your brother's face
I see you
            YES   I really do see you right now
I see you when I close my eyes
            and when they are opened
Isn't it enough already?
            After nine years I still see you clearly

For Jigme the Cat at the Bardo Gate

Blessed are they who die in the beauty of their time
Blessed the ones who die without process
who die in a moment of laughter
or a sudden opening of the great heart
they are blessed who never know
the fat sucked from their eyes or breath hot and foul
a body drops away ever so slowly
pain envelopes the senses
the eye forgets how to see and slides crooked and white
an inner thunder numbs the ears
everything that was soft becomes dry
everything that was sharp falls without power
nothing holds its shape
nothing remains
Dissolution Dissolution

O friend and companion of 14 years
I offer you water but you reject me
your ears no longer turn to my voice
your jeweled yellow eyes are lost
This morning you asked for the warmth of my body
and nuzzled my arm inhaling softly
Now bright day you hide away and refuse to know me

Even rejected I will sit with you at the gates of the bardo
and ring the bronze bell when you cross.

103 Moons Knob Hill

To: Hylocichla@

Rain sinking into snow
the blue wind laughs between spruce trees
in the night it roars and roars
all the terrors of the world dissipate
like oil shine in the gray tide
the wind purifies us
leaving only torn alder leaves
and wisps of spruce beard
like love letters in the morning snow
OM MANI PADME HUNG
So ha!

112 Moons Knob Hill

for Chong An

Sun on yellow grass
sandhill cranes call their mates and dance
wind like cool wine
great silence/ blue space
white glaciers
the sea is a silver blanket thrown carelessly
across the sky
I am drunk with time zones
bones chilled   fingers warmed in sun
confused senses   time   space
what is it all anyway?
                    and who am I to ask?
I'll just sit hear until I hear the bell
ringing somewhere in the nightless sky

116 Moons
returned from Korea

Look Again!

I am seed-intention-opening
my garden-mind   a hologram
of bright winds

There are no gates opened or closed
no path to follow
and every flower I see   I see
everywhere

Trusting the turns of the way   the blooming
galaxies call their golden bees
blue poppies grow from my fingers
offering them naturally
to you and you

The trees of childhood grow roots from my toes
words are clear running over pale stones
no way to stop them
too slippery to hold
but cool and sweet in the throat

My every-eye gardens in all directions
If you are not in the garden ...
Look again !

118 Moons Knob Hill

Himachal Lice

I am not alone   my head is full
of consciousness
I can feel all that MIND
as it were my own   but it is not
my head is occupied
by tiny desires   I would never have

Why do I listen to them?
how can they make me feel
SO SAD
I open the poison and think
Just one more day
This life I am living   is it real?

A few days of silence
and then
the whispering begins again

O India, land of my ancestors' birth
o the stories I have heard
of life   of life
        irrepressible !

118 moons Knob Hill

Red Death

An hour before dawn   sleepless
I think   there is no path
          from my bed to the trees
No Path!   and the tall ferns   like green waves
     rise and fall   rise and fall

The bark of the spruce forest has become my skin
I don't know where I am   or who
torn to the edge by these years of buried love
The taste of resin fills my blood
     I smell the slow red fire creeping near

A web of strong roots holds these mountains down
holds the great winds in the sky
These roots   but earth is soft as spruce needles
     how can they hold when minerals and memory retreat?

An hour before dawn in cold blue light
thrushes' songs echo deep among the dying trees
like bamboo flutes   not sweet   not mournful
     dark bells inside the hills   calling everyone

300 years standing   these trees   these ancient birds
now red-gray branches   a lacework of death
from valley to ridge
     a slow fire consumes us all
          consumes us all

118 moons Knob Hill

Tenth Year October

In salt-wet sand
           a handsome footprint
                halts my steps

Waves have erased
           the walking line
             of these strong feet

Now
only this single
           high-arched footprint

steps into
           unbroken light

Salt tears suddenly cloud my eyes
I am filled with deep longing
as if
      I were seeing
                the last step
                   just taken
                        by my own
                           dear one

121 Moons

email poem
"And You Will Teach Me to Breathe Perfume Into the Wings of Butterflies"

Oh, will I ?
instead I ask you
who breathes the essence of flowers
who speaks sap and soil
whose tongue rolls to whistle
what only the sycamore hears?

The butterfly rises on wings
as thin as passing thoughts
the veins of her wings are hollow
but only the perfumed breath of flowers
in the wildest dreams of hummingbirds
is light enough to dwell there

You are only an august flower in the wind
rooted in a fantasy of flight
your petaled words,
wingless like prayer flags
       tugging on cold mountain wind

131 moons

Meconopsis

An evening-blue poppy opens
shedding its green pod
fully ripe with yearning
no time wasted   just being pretty

cold winds blow even in mid-summer

Among the violet-blue petals
a swollen stamen
powdered with sweetened gold
invites

142 moons Knob Hill

Wrangle Mountains late August

In an abandoned river channel
          away from the glacial torrent
my white tent stands lonely among willows
its nylon door faces   sky between mountains
sleeping on my belly   head near the door

In the pale night   piercing a dream   I hear
a branch snap
every synapse of my mind is aroused
eyes open   head turns to the sound

a full silver moon illuminates the tent wall
and across this thin fabric   a shadow passes
blocking the moon
                    blocking the moon
a dark shadow passes without another sound
every hair on her shoulder hump clearly numbered
the long body glides across my screen
          and the moon   returns
the brilliant moon
                    returns
I breathe again   softly

between the mountains   green fire
bursts across the sky
pulsing curtains of willow colored light

delicious peace enfolds me
wrapped in a blanket of green aurora
I sleep deeply without fear

143 moons

81

Glaciers and Rocks

I am just listening on a boulder
Breathing and listening to the music
of glacial motion

Guggel plop glug glug glug

tinkle PLOP! tinkle

S s i s i s h s i s c h e tinkle

gug guggel   plunch

PLOP!

O Basho, your frogs can
never sing so sweetly
These melodious plops!

In a circle of multi-colored glacial till
Hills that are not hills crawl slowly past me
Their bones transient ice seeking
To ascend the water cycle path
Once more

Think how long this ice has been ice
Working to carve valleys
Now coming back to sun   air
Free at last of its rocky burdens
The sun calls ice home
The wind invites ice to fly

My breath joins glacier's breath
to ascend the sky

143 Moons

Hallo Bay

After a day of walking in sea mud lowest solstice tide
watching bears the size of bulls graze on clams
fording an icy river in leaky boots
the warm afternoon sun   windless bugless
a paradise of silence from man
there in the sweet sedge grass I see
the great bear mother   teats to the sky
in calm relaxation   napping with a cub
her golden sun warmed fur in the green grass
I feel the power of sleep calling me
how lovely to lie down with mother
and let my day weary eyes close with hers
who can imagine the dreams we might share?

O my lost one
knowing how you also love mother
I left your tiny bone in an Aleutian garden

201 Moons

83

I am waiting for peace

1949
There are three things I fear
bears in the closet, dinosaurs looking in my third floor window
and when I see a plane over the city
I ask,   Mommy are the Russians going to bomb us?

I am waiting for peace

1953
PS 41. we practice duck and cover
our thin wooden desks as shields against nuclear bombs
sometimes the whole school practices Bomb Drills
gathering in straight silent lines, it seems like hours, legs hurting
in the cold basement we don't know what "practice" means

I am waiting for peace, waiting

1959
I stand with a group of women, vigil to end segregation
6th avenue traffic swirls around us
somewhere in the South people are beaten
the florist from across the street tearfully brings us red carnations

I am waiting, waiting for peace

1961
With 20,000 people chanting Ban the Bomb
our voices fill all space, we are joyous
our bodies block traffic in Times Square
we chant NO MORE BOMBS
At the UN Plaza Pete Seeger sings to us
We will Study War No More Down By The River Side,
We Will Overcome, Yes!
In my 15 year old heart I know it will be true
but the New York Times next day has only a small mention

I am waiting for peace, for peace

1962
All day in school we wait for war, some of us wear brave faces
we sing Cuba Cuba, Cuba si, Yankee no
war does not come

But I am still waiting for peace

1963
Paris France, On a boat on the Seine the radio announces
President Kennedy is dead. The world weeps.

Numb with shock, what am I waiting for

1966
I am marching to Oakland with Country Joe and the Fish
singing One, Two, Three , Four, What are we waiting for,
don't ask me I don't give a damn, next stop is Vietnam

The Oakland police tear-gas us and we scatter
I am choking to breathe, I am choking back tears
Don't police protect people ?

I am confused, but still waiting for peace

1967
We feel strong. Our colors showing fearlessly
January 14th A Gathering of The Tribes in Golden Gate Park
We BE IN all day in great happiness, LOVE is
Allen Ginsberg, Gary Snyder, Timothy Leary, Jerry Ruben,
Lenore Kandel poets, politicos, The Grateful Dead
Hells Angels guard us and harmony flowers
Leaving the park there are fire engines, police cars, chaos
but the day is still within us   and we only smile

I can feel peace coming . . soon

1967
Taos, New Mexico building a home for New Buffalo
we will grow everything with love
But on LOVE we don't agree.
If together it is difficult, is it possible alone?

I am tired of waiting for everything

1968
Martin Luther King assassinated, Robert Kennedy shot dead !
I feel the forces of Mordor rising against us

Dare I hope   for peace ?

1969
Leaving everyone for Alaska
two years alone in deep snow, five years
with a very wrong man
I discover mindless rage
like War it comes in a flash
with better aim
I   might have been a murderer

I watch my mind for portents of peace

1979
The Dalai Lama holds my hand
Feeling peace near the tree and being a leaf
are not the same

2013
Where is peace? I have waited, hoped, practiced
I can only change myself

Second World War, Korean War, Vietnam War, Gulf War,
9/11, Afghanistan and . .
war breeds war, war   breeds   war

I weep for us-the-planet, our shared mother-body-mind

Om Mani Padme Hung !

Bellingham, Washington 2013

Story

It was Paljor's day off from work on October 25, 1988, full moon day. But soon after we woke up the telephone rang and the dispatcher from the Longshoreman's Union asked Paljor to come to work. Longshoring was his second job, usually once but sometimes twice a week. I made oatmeal for breakfast. Paljor asked me to make Lasagna for dinner and then he left for the docks. From the window I saw him sitting in his truck letting the engine warm up. I had a geology test at the college and then had to pick up some papers from work. All morning I was apprehensive. During my test I was thinking of Paljor and then driving home as the light turned green at Fireweed Lane and I headed down the hill, I heard the words of an old song in my mind.

> ". . . his head was found neath the driver's wheel but his body
> it never was found . . ." (In The Pines, traditional folk song.)

Suddenly I *saw* huge semi-truck tires and Paljor's voice said clearly, *"those tires won't hurt me, Oh yes they will."* I felt a wave of love from him. I wanted to go to the docks but my intuition, told me he wasn't there. I turned down the street to go home but suddenly decided to visit our neighbor Marilyn. I drank tea with her husband, Bill, who told me stories of his life on the Stikine River. He loved to tell stories and it was difficult to leave. At last I could no longer delay going home. When I got out of my car Mark was waiting for me, but he only said Paljor had had an *accident* and was in the hospital. I threw down my school books and asked which hospital, but Mark insisted he would drive me. There are three hospitals in Anchorage, we went to two of them and didn't find Paljor, which made me very uneasy, then we went to the Alaska Native Hospital, the one closest to the Port. The emergency desk said he was with the doctor and I had to wait. I insisted I had to see him so they led me, not to a room, but down a dark hallway and into an small cluttered office. Then I heard the words, like in a movie. *"We did everything we could . . . "* For a long moment the words made no sense. Things moved in slow-motion and I felt as if I were underwater.

I wanted to see him. The man didn't *recommend it*, but I knew I must. In the morgue, they pulled a drawer out of the wall, and inside a body was wrapped in a white sheet. Just my husband's face was visible. I wasn't allowed to unwrap him. His body was empty, but it was a body I knew very well. I said prayers in his ears. We left. Mark drove me home still clinging to Paljor's work boots. Time stopped. When evening came I was alarmed that the shy changed color. I was waiting for Paljor to return.

Paljor was born in Western Tibet and spent the first part of his life as a Buddhist monk. His family fled to India when the Communist Chinese invaded Tibet in 1959. After graduating high school in India he went to a Buddhist university in Thailand and from there got a job as a translator for Nechung Rinpoche in Hawaii. Rinpoche and Paljor were invited to Fairbanks, Alaska to give a dharma teaching in 1977 and it was then that Paljor decided he wanted to live in Alaska, a land of high snowy mountains and wide rivers.

I was born in the New York City art world and after many adventures ended up in Alaska in 1969. I lived alone in the woods for several years, lived with an enchanted bear for a few years, worked on the Trans-Alaska Pipeline as a laborer, and then escaping from the bear, moved to Anchorage in 1977. Paljor and I met in 1978 and in the spring of 1979 we got married. With several friends we started Khawachen Dharma Center and the Alaska Tibet Committee, bringing Tibetan Lamas to teach Buddhism, and working to educate people about what was happening in Tibet. We were planning to have children.

Paljor was crushed under the wheels of a semi truck and he died at the Port of Anchorage. It was an *accident*. That word still vibrates in my mind. After Paljor's death I moved from the city to live alone in a small cabin near Homer, and it is there many of these poems were written. Because it was full moon when Paljor died I have numbered the poems by the moon. It is only now, 28 years since his death that I am ready to let them all go out in the world. Some have been published alone, but I feel the natural order of these lived-poems together tell the full story of my journey. I lived in vast Alaska with cold wind, stars, aurora, salmon, bears, and deep snow. These poems do not lie, whatever story they tell, I did. I do not use words describing nature to attempt to be *spiritual*. I don't make a distinction between ordinary reality and special reality. Paljor was very fond of saying *Life in Nirvana is boring without Samsara.* When your truck is stuck a mile from home in three feet of snow on a steep icy road with wind blasting snow grains in your eyes, your gloves vanish while trying to put on chains and fingers freeze. Then climbing the hill, besides groceries you have to carry a hysterical 12 pound cat while the neighbor's dogs dance around, that might be called Samsara. Nirvana is realizing at this moment of suffering that the light of the storm has a brilliant energy and the situation is really funny. There is no space between Samsara and Nirvana, a complete interdependence unites everything we perceive as separate.

This book is dedicated to Ngodup Paljor, my husband and teacher, to my parents Ibram and Ernestine Lassaw, and many other dear friends, including Mark Reiss, who have gone on before me. And to all sentient beings who each experience suffering and grief. And it is dedicated to my dear friend, Serge Lecomte.

Please read *Songs of a Wild Yak*, a collection of Paljor's poems.

Bio Note

Denise Lassaw grew up in the New York art world. Living and traveling in many places on the planet, including Mongolia, India, Nepal, Europe, and in California during the 60s, she spent a winter in a teepee in New Mexico, taught papier mâché mask making and puppets to Inuit children in the arctic, worked as a laborer on the Trans-Alaska Pipeline, did construction work in Anchorage, taught ceramics, sold welded belt buckles and necklaces at craft fairs; and lived alone in the wilds of Alaska, making everything she needed by hand. She has published her poetry and essays on life and art in various places, given a slide talk at the National Portrait Gallery, written a script for a film about Tibet, and had many sweet adventures. There is no way to write a short bio without telling stories that become longer and longer. It is easier to say what she did not do: get a fancy college degree; have a full time job for years and years, remain in one place, have a mortgage; or wear high heels more than once in her life. It is enough to say she has created her own life and despite being completely human, is happy.

Publication History

In addition to *The Widow's Book of Moons*, Denise Lassaw has contributed essays on the work of her late father, sculptor Ibram Lassaw, for national and international catalogs, worked as a copy-editor for art historians and graduate students, gave a lecture on Elaine de Kooning at the National Portrait Gallery, consulted for museums doing shows on abstract expressionism, and written a film, *Tibet: A Moment in Time* for film maker William Bacon. Lassaw has published poems in various small magazines and in several publications such as *What Book?! Buddha Poems from Beat to Hip Hop*, edited by Gary Gach. She has participated in poetry readings from New York to San Francisco and from Alaska to Korea and India. In 2016 she published *Songs of a Wild Yak* by Ngodup Paljor, her late husband.

Future projects which are already underway include a Catalogue Raisonné on Ibram Lassaw and a book about growing up in the New York art world of the 50s.

Made in the USA
San Bernardino, CA
22 January 2017